GORILLA VS. LEOPARD

BY NATHAN SOMMER

BELLWETHER MEDIA • MINNEAPOLIS, MN

Torque brims with excitement
perfect for thrill-seekers of all kinds.
Discover daring survival skills, explore
uncharted worlds, and marvel at mighty
engines and extreme sports. In *Torque* books,
anything can happen. Are you ready?

This edition first published in 2020 by Bellwether Media, Inc.

No part of this publication may be reproduced in whole or in part without
written permission of the publisher.
For information regarding permission, write to Bellwether Media, Inc.,
Attention: Permissions Department,
6012 Blue Circle Drive, Minnetonka, MN 55343.

Library of Congress Cataloging-in-Publication Data

Names: Sommer, Nathan, author.
Title: Gorilla vs. Leopard / by Nathan Sommer.
   Other titles: Gorilla versus leopard
Description: Minneapolis, MN : Bellwether Media, Inc., 2020. | Series:
   Torque: animal battles | Includes bibliographical references and index.
   | Audience: Ages 7-12 | Audience: Grades 3-7 | Summary: "Amazing
   photography accompanies engaging information about gorillas and
   leopards. The combination of high-interest subject matter and light text
   is intended for students in grades 3 through 7"– Provided by publisher.
Identifiers: LCCN 2019030404 (print) | LCCN 2019030405 (ebook) | ISBN
   9781644871560 (library binding) | ISBN 9781618918369 (ebook)
Subjects: LCSH: Gorilla–Juvenile literature. | Leopard–Juvenile literature.
Classification: LCC QL737.P94 S66 2020 (print) | LCC QL737.P94 (ebook) |
   DDC 599.884–dc23
LC record available at https://lccn.loc.gov/2019030404
LC ebook record available at https://lccn.loc.gov/2019030405

Editor: Christina Leaf   Designer: Andrea Schneider

Printed in the United States of America, North Mankato, MN.

TABLE OF CONTENTS

THE COMPETITORS

Who rules the jungle? It is easy to choose gorillas. They are the largest **primates**. The powerful giants are also unbelievably smart.

But gorillas may have met their match in leopards. These graceful big cats are some of the fiercest hunters in the wild. It is an epic battle when these two animals face off!

Gorillas have sturdy bodies with wide chests and human-like hands. The beasts mostly use their long arms to walk on all fours. But they can stand when they have to.

Gorillas are found in the thick **rain forests** of Africa. The apes usually live in groups of up to 30. They can eat around 40 pounds (18.1 kilograms) of food per day!

GORILLA PROFILE

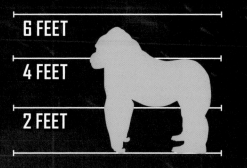

6 FEET

4 FEET

2 FEET

HEIGHT
UP TO 5.5 FEET
(1.7 METERS)

WEIGHT
UP TO 485 POUNDS
(220 KILOGRAMS)

HABITAT

RAIN FORESTS

JUNGLES

GORILLA RANGE

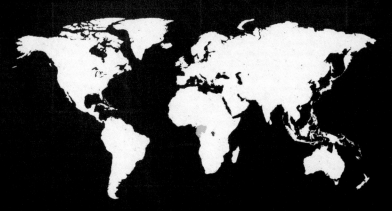

WESTERN GORILLA RANGE ■
EASTERN GORILLA RANGE ■

LEOPARD PROFILE

BODY LENGTH
UP TO 7 FEET (2.1 METERS)

| 0 | 2 FEET | 4 FEET | 6 FEET | 8 FEET |

WEIGHT
UP TO 200 POUNDS (90 KILOGRAMS)

HABITAT

RAIN FORESTS   MOUNTAINS   PLAINS   DESERTS

LEOPARD RANGE

■ RANGE

WATER-LOVING CATS

Unlike most cats, leopards are expert swimmers. They use this skill to catch prey in water.

Leopards have long bodies with short legs. The nine **subspecies** of leopard have slightly different coats. Each is covered in dark spots called **rosettes**.

Leopards live in many **habitats**. They prefer rain forests, jungles, and grasslands. The big cats also roam deserts and mountains. Unlike gorillas, these **nocturnal** hunters live alone.

SECRET WEAPONS

Rosettes **camouflage** leopards well. The cats lay low in thick grass before they pounce on **prey**. These expert climbers also blend in atop tree branches.

Gorillas use fur to their **advantage**, too. Silver patches on males' backs make them seem larger. This helps scare off threats.

SILVER
PATCHES

TOOL MASTERS

Gorillas are very smart and can learn to use tools. A gorilla has been seen using a stick to tell how deep water is. Another has been seen using bamboo shoots as a ladder!

SECRET WEAPONS

SPOTTED FUR

SHARP TEETH

SHARP CLAWS

MUSCULAR LEGS

CANINE TOOTH

Long **canine teeth** help leopards bring down prey. These teeth are up to 1.5 inches (3.6 centimeters) long. The cats also have piercing claws. These cut through skin to injure prey.

Gorillas have big canines as well. They mostly use these to frighten attackers and males that are a threat. But these teeth give gorillas a powerful bite!

SECRET WEAPONS

GORILLA

STRONG ARMS

SILVER FUR

LONG CANINE TEETH

TOP SPEED

36 MILES (58 KILOMETERS) PER HOUR

LEOPARD

28 MILES (45 KILOMETERS) PER HOUR

HUMAN

Leopards have muscular legs. They reach speeds of 36 miles (58 kilometers) per hour. These **predators** can jump 10 feet (3 meters) high. They can leap distances of 20 feet (6.1 meters)!

Scientists believe gorillas are up to eight times stronger than humans. They think the apes can lift up to 1,800 pounds (815 kilograms). That is heavier than a fishing boat!

MAX STRENGTH

ATTACK MOVES

Leopards **ambush** enemies by hiding and **stalking** them. These hunters lay in wait until the perfect moment. Then they attack enemies with sharp teeth and claws.

Gorillas are mostly peaceful. But they will fight if threatened! Males scream loudly to warn their groups when danger appears. They beat their chests and charge forward to scare off attackers

Leopards have powerful jaws. These can break the necks of enemies in one bite. This **paralyzes** their attackers. Another bite to the

Gorillas use weight to their advantage. They may pin enemies to the ground. Strong arms and legs can give powerful blows. A bite from their huge canine teeth does a lot of damage, too!

READY, FIGHT!

A gorilla notices a leopard waiting to ambush. It roars, pounding the ground in anger. The gorilla's show does not scare away the crafty leopard.

The leopard leaps and bites the gorilla's neck. The gorilla smacks away the leopard, but enough damage is done. The injured gorilla runs away in pain. Leopards are the jungle champions today!

GLOSSARY

advantage—something an animal has or can do better than their enemy

ambush—to carry out a surprise attack

camouflage—to use colors and patterns to help an animal hide in its surroundings

canine teeth—long, pointed teeth that are often the sharpest in the mouth

habitats—the homes or areas where animals prefer to live

nocturnal—active at night

paralyzes—makes something unable to move

predators—animals that hunt other animals for food

prey—animals that are hunted by other animals for food

primates—any of a group of mammals that includes humans, apes, and monkeys

rain forests—thick, green forests that receive a lot of rain

rosettes—the spots on a leopard

stalking—following slowly and quietly

subspecies—particular types of animals that exist within a species

TO LEARN MORE

AT THE LIBRARY

Jones, Elton. *Gorillas Work Together*. New York, N.Y.: PowerKids Press, 2018.

Krieger, Emily. *Animal Smackdown: Surprising Animal Matchups with Surprising Results*. Washington, D.C.: National Geographic Kids, 2018.

Mills, Andrea. *Big Cats*. New York, N.Y.: DK Publishing, 2019.

ON THE WEB

FACTSURFER

Factsurfer.com gives you a safe, fun way to find more information.

1. Go to www.factsurfer.com

2. Enter "gorilla vs. leopard" into the search box and click 🔍.

3. Select your book cover to see a list of related web sites.

INDEX

The images in this book are reproduced through the courtesy of: Minikhan, front cover (gorilla); The Len, front cover (leopard); GR92100 p. 4; StuPorts, p. 5; Alan Tunnicliffe, pp. 6-7, 19; Volodymyr Burdiak, pp. 8-9; Maryke Scheun, p. 10; Mike Price, p. 11; Villiers Steyn, p. 12 (leopard); Lee Elvin, p. 12 (weapon 1); JoanneJean, p. 12 (weapon 2); Eliot Lasnier/ Getty Images, p. 12 (weapon 3); Viju Jose, p. 12 (weapon 4); hpbdesign, p. 13 (gorilla); Jiri Foltyn, p. 13 (weapon 1); PaulSat, p. 13 (weapon 2); Frank Cornelissen, p. 13 (weapon 3); Arco Images GMbH/ Alamy, p. 14; Nataly Reinch, p. 15; Ercan Uc, p. 16; National Geographic Image Collection/ Alamy, p. 17; Robert L. Sanson, p. 18; mlharing, p. 20 (leopard); CherylRamalho, pp. 20-21 (gorilla); Quickshot, pp. 20-21 (background).